The Covert Manipulator

How to Stealthily Get Inside of Anyone's Mind

By Ben Gaston

Published by Make Profits Easy LLC

Profitsdaily123@aol.com

facebook.com/MakeProfitsEasy

Table of Contents

Introduction

The most powerful person in the world is not some brutal dictator who took his power through brute force. The most powerful person in the world is not the business tycoon or appointed monarch who inherited money and success. The most powerful person in the world is not the greatest genius, or richest heir, or most popular politician or celebrity. These people do hold power, but they are not the most powerful of all people.

No, the most powerful person in the world is the covert manipulator. Because the covert manipulator can get whatever he wants, whenever he wants it. Without shame, he can enter the minds of others and influence them in the direction that he wants. He wears many masks, so no one can ever catch him at his act. He gets away with murder, metaphorically of course.

You can become the most powerful person in the world. This book will show you how. This book is crammed with tips on how to become a covert manipulator. In these pages, you will learn how to make sure that nothing ever stops you from getting what you desire. You can have anything in the world if you learn how to manipulate others. You will also be able to control people and mold them into what you want.

This book will also show you how to spot and thwart covert manipulators who work on you. Manipulators take away your power. Subverting their attempts helps preserve your power and dignity. You should always be two steps ahead of any manipulator.

So what is the appeal of manipulation? What's the point of it? Well, manipulation is the process of using people. You can use people to achieve various aims that you may have. Since people may not always be willing to help you, you can use manipulation to make them say yes to you. You can also use manipulation to make people feel or think in certain ways that benefits you.

Manipulation has a really negative connotation. People who manipulate are considered bad people. Manipulation is an ethical no-no. Yet almost everyone has used manipulation at some point in their lives, in some way. Some people are more manipulative than others, but almost everyone has figured out that manipulation is the easiest way to get things done sometimes. You are not a bad person for using the techniques covered in this book.

You must also understand that manipulation can be used for any purpose. It does not have to be used for evil purposes. Just because you learn manipulation tactics and develop some manipulative tendencies after reading this book does not mean that you are a super villain, out to hurt people. Manipulation is just a way to work people and situations to serve your needs. It's really just self-preservation and ingenuity. The world's greatest politicians are super manipulators, for instance. Their goals are not always evil, but they know how to get people to do what they want.

But you need to be careful. Otherwise, no one will have any desire to do things for you and they will avoid associating with you. You will blow the trust and faith of others if you are caught using manipulation. So that is why you must be a covert manipulator. The whole theme of this book is teaching you how to manipulate while being covert about it. Covert means that you work under a cover, that you're sneaky and stealthy. You want to manipulate others without getting caught. This book will show you how to operate in stealth mode.

Chapter 1: The Basics of Manipulation

Manipulation is a delicate art. There are countless ways to use it. This book cannot possibly cover every single way, but we will cover some of the major tactics that you absolutely must know. From there, you can start to learn how to take advantage of situations as you see fit. You will learn how to work people in your own special style.

In this chapter, we will visit several basic methods that lay the groundwork for more advanced techniques. These basic techniques will work on their own quite well, however. In later chapters, we will delve into more specific and advanced methods of manipulation.

Get to Know Someone

There is no way to run manipulation on someone successfully without first knowing a few things about your subject. You want to find out some key facts that enable you to crawl into both his mind and heart. Only then can you start working your manipulative magic.

First, you want to find out what someone really wants out of his life. Find out his desires, hopes, and dreams. Find out what makes him smile and what makes him get up out of bed in the mornings. His passions and his hopes are driving things that mean a lot to him. Therefore, they have a huge impact on his emotional well-being. That makes them useful tools for your manipulation.

Next, find out what he loves. Find out the people and things that he holds dear in his heart. These things mean the world to him. You can use them to reward him or threaten him.

Find out what he is guilty of. Guilt is a super powerful emotion that people hate feeling. If you use guilt, you can drive someone to action. So find out bad things that he has done in the past. He might look sad when he does not do well at work, so you know that his work ethic drives him and he feels guilty when he fails or is lazy.

Also find out what he hates about himself, or what he is insecure about. If he is balding, and keeps his scalp covered with a scarf or hat, then he might be self-conscious about his baldness and you can use that to hurt him. If he is reluctant to speak to women, you can guess that he is shy and probably insecure about his social skills.

You can find out what someone likes sexually, as well. Sexuality is a huge motivator for a lot of people. If you can tempt someone with sex somehow, you can often get results. Use sex as a manipulation tool. Learn what turns him on and what you can do to get him to perform actions to get laid.

Finally, find out what really, really irritates him. Sometimes you can drive someone to do what you want just so that you stop irritating him. Find out what pushes him into anger. Then keep that knowledge in your back pocket for when you really need to goad him or provoke him.

Emotional Manipulation

Emotional manipulation involves playing with someone's emotions, making them take the action or draw the conclusion that you desire. There are many ways to play with someone's emotions for control. Emotional manipulation is often very successful because emotions drive people. You can influence one's thoughts and actions with emotional manipulation. Making someone feel something is essential to emotional manipulation, but you also want to make someone rely on you for relief of negative emotions or for positive emotions.

Fear-then-Relief

The first and most important method of emotional manipulation is called fear-then-relief. It is exactly what it sounds like. First you trigger a fear response in someone. Then you offer them the key to relief. You create a bad emotion that you also offer recovery from. Your subject will become reliant upon you in order to stop whatever scares him.

There are a variety of ways to accomplish fear. One way is to introduce him to someone who might make a move on his wife or girlfriend, or his job, or something else that he cherishes. Expose him to people who threaten what he loves and hopes for. Offer to somehow protect him from this person or offer him comfort and tell him that he won't lose what he cherishes. Advise him on how to deal with this problematic person in his life.

If you know that he is already jealous of someone or threatened by someone, you can irritate that jealousy some more. Talk innocently about how fantastic this person is at work or how great he looks so that your subject feels even more threatened by him.

You can also accomplish this by exposing him to evidence that what he loves might be taken away. For instance, you might tell him that you overheard the boss talking about laying him off. Use what he loves against him. Then offer him relief or some sort of saving grace.

You can also threaten him directly, but this is not so covert. You can be discreet and pretend like you don't know that you are threatening him. Then offer him relief by revealing that you won't actually take anything from him or telling him that he has nothing to fear about you. But you are still putting yourself in the line of fire when you pose any sort of threat to him yourself. Think very carefully before you make yourself any sort of threat to your subject. It is far more covert and sneaky to use other people to threaten him. You appear more innocent when you do this.

Guilt

No one likes the aching, terrible feeling of guilt. Using guilt is a great way to make someone do what you want. When you make him feel guilty, he will do pretty much anything to get rid of the feeling. That puts him in a very malleable spot where you can influence him strongly.

There are a few ways to use guilt. The most obvious is to make someone feel guilty for not doing something for you. You can bring up something bad that he did in the past and tell him, "Why won't you do this for me when you hurt me in the past? You do owe me, you know. This is your chance to make things right."

You can use guilt to make him hate himself and to lower his self-esteem. Bring up things that he is ashamed of or guilty over. If he is currently guilty of something, such as a crime, not taking care of himself, cheating on his significant other, etc., you can hold that over his head and make him feel like a horrible person. Or bring up things from his past to chip away at his sense of self-worth.

You can even use guilt to make someone feel responsible for something that is not even his fault really. Somehow twist the situation so that he looks responsible. Tell him that he is at fault, even if you have to lie. Guilt will weigh on him and he may feel that he owes you.

Make him feel horrible for doing something small. It may not be a big deal what he did, but you can blow it up out of proportion so that he feels terrible about it. Show how deeply and profoundly he hurt you. Maybe say that what he did reminds you of a horrible event from your childhood. This can work in the smallest of situations, like if he is playing a song you don't like. You can tell him, "That song brings back horrible memories. Please don't ever play it around me again." You can even cry a little for extra effect, or fly into a panic attack and blame him for triggering it.

Finally, you can use guilt as a form of blackmailing. Emotional blackmailing always plays on guilt. Threaten to expose him for how awful he truly is. Tell him that he is a horrible person and you will expose him to his loved ones or friends. If you have any dirt on him, you can use that for your blackmail to work best.

Reciprocity

Reciprocity is the art of making someone feel as if he owes you. Basically, you want to do someone a favor. Get your foot in the door by performing something for him that he needs or wants. He will naturally want to reciprocate. You can call on him to do something for you eventually, and bring up what you did for him to get him to agree to do it.

You can use reciprocity to get people to do things for you or to say yes to you. You use a combination of warmth and guilt. By doing him a favor, you warm him up to you. But you also make him feel guilty if he doesn't say yes.

Emotional Roller Coaster

First you make someone feel really good. You groom him over time to rely on you for feeling good. Your flattery makes him feel so great that he wants to spend lots of time around you because you stroke his ego. Over time, he learns to associate you with good feelings so he turns to you for emotional gratification when he's feeling down. This puts him in a vulnerable place, because now he relies on you. He has no clue that you are secretly the enemy that he should beware of.

Then, you let him down. You make him feel horrible about himself. He will turn to you for comfort and reassurance, even though you just hurt him. He will want to return to the times when you had only compliments and flattery, so he will strive to please you.

Being unpredictable in your moods can really keep him on his toes. Being happy at one moment and upset the next will make him scramble to keep you happy. He won't know what he did wrong. He may even feel like a terrible person for letting you down or upsetting you. You can make him work hard to please you and keep you in a good mood where you don't lash out at him.

Use Sex as a Tool

Sex is a super powerful means by which you can manipulate someone. People are strongly driven by the instinctual desire to have sex. They are also strongly driven by the desire to look good to whichever gender they are attracted to and to be sexually pleasing. You can use both instincts to your advantage.

Obviously, seducing someone is a good way to get him to do what you want. You can make him jump through hoops and work to please you in order to get laid by you. Women often use this seduction method and show off their breasts or speak in a sexy voice or wave around their hair to make men do what they want. They use their sexual partners for various needs, ranging from emotional to material. Men also use the promise of sex to get their partners to do what they want, though usually to a lesser extent.

But what if you can't seduce someone? Maybe he isn't your type, or he isn't someone that you could have sex with or want to have sex with. Maybe he is a family member or of the gender that you don't desire. In that case, you can still use sex by tempting him with other people. You might offer to let him meet an attractive person that you know if he does something for you, for instance.

You can also play with his confidence in his appearance and sex appeal. A large part of a person's ego is based on how attractive other people find him or her. Some people have given up on being attractive, so sexual manipulation may not work on such people. But people who are very vain, who express desperation in finding a romantic partner, who strive to look good and stay fit, or who admit to having body image issues are weak to this type of manipulation. Use their sexual attractiveness to bolster their ego and their lack of attractiveness to bring them down. If you are in a relationship with someone, you can gain control over him/her by making him/her feel as if no one else could possibly find him/her attractive. Then he or she will want to stay with you, since you at least want to be in the relationship and no one else would.

Language

Language is incredibly powerful, in a hypnotic, hidden way. The way you word what you say has a huge impact on how someone responds. You can choose certain words to change someone's mood or influence someone's response and subsequent actions.

Passive Language

To avoid taking responsibility for something, you can refer to things in the passive tense. "The door was left unlocked" makes you sound less guilty than if you say "I left the door unlocked." You can really shirk off a lot of responsibility by speaking about your actions in a more passive way.

You can also make someone feel more or less responsible by using the passive tense. Let's say you want to make someone feel bad for failing to do something at work, but you don't want to directly confront him. You can circumvent a confrontation by saying, "Since this did not get done yesterday, some of you are going to have extra work today. Remember to always complete your daily tasks on time." This vague wording makes you seem like less of a jerk, but it still shows the subject of your frustration that he messed up and you know it.

Remove the brevity from situations by using more passive language, as well. If someone is freaking out at you over something that you did, you can use the passive language and more passive word choices to lower the seriousness of what you did. Calm him down by choosing words that carry less weight. For instance, if someone is mad at you for lying, you can insist that you simply left out a detail or that you colored the facts. These euphemisms for lying will actually make him feel a little less miffed about your deception.

Context

Even if you stay within the proper context of your conversation, you can choose phrases that make the person think of something else. Choose language that refers to another subject while pretending to be talking about something. Double entendres is one way to accomplish this. Another way is to simply speak about a situation that is very similar to a more personal situation you may share with this person.

Say you are mad at someone for leaving your cat out. So you pretend to talk about his irresponsibility at work, but you keep bringing up how he doesn't take care of things. Tell him how serious his negligence is. Maybe slip in a cat reference where it fits. This lets him know that you are angry about what he did to your cat. Meanwhile, you never directly tell him how you feel.

Another example: you are having a professional conversation with a co-worker, but you are trying to earn his favor by being mildly seductive. You can put sex onto his mind by making sexual innuendos that also relate to the subject matter of your conversation.

Happy or Sad Words

You can influence someone's mood by how you speak. You can communicate the same message, but depending on the words and tone that you use, you can convey different moods. Using tone, word choice, and body language, you can show someone how to feel.

Say someone is excited about a new person that he met. You can congratulate him, but seem skeptical in your body language and facial expression. He will want to know what's wrong with the girl. Say, "Nothing...." as if there is more that you won't tell him. This will discourage him from dating the girl because he will be riddled with doubt about her.

Or you can say yes when someone asks you to do something. But say yes in a very discourage or unhappy way. He will sense that you don't really want to do it.

You can tell someone happy news in a sad way to ruin his joy. Or you can tell him sad news in a happy way to lessen the impact that the news has on his mood.

Unsettle Someone

The best way to make someone an easy target for manipulation is to move him into a vulnerable position. You want to disrupt his comfort zone. He will do anything to return to that comfort zone, so he will be in a place where you can really pack a punch on his mind.

Isolation

Once you get someone out of his comfort zone, you tear away his support. He becomes reliant solely on you. He also doesn't defend himself as well.

There are several ways to isolate someone. The first way is to isolate him mentally. Take away the things that he relies on to validate his thoughts. You may take away his favorite book or limit his access to the Internet, for instance, so that he doesn't have his favorite sources of information. Remove his safety blanket, so to speak, by removing his access to things that he relies on for comfort and support.

You can isolate him socially. As you make his friends and family hate him by embarrassing him, you remove his social support. You can also convince him that his friends and family are not good for him and provide convincing evidence so that he stops talking to the people whom he loves. Without social support, he has no one to bolster his self-esteem or to reaffirm his self-image. No one can protect him or tell him that you are bad for him. He is completely alone and needy of you.

Finally, you can physically isolate him. Get him somewhere away from his home, his office, and even his car. Make sure that the surroundings are completely unfamiliar. Then he will feel less at ease. He might be more open to saying yes to you or acting out of character. He also will probably be less able to defend himself against you should you say mean things to him. Just putting him in a completely unfamiliar situation can disarm him and make him incredibly uneasy.

Discredit Him

Your subject is most likely sensitive about his reputation. He wants to look good to others. So if you ruin his reputation, you put him in a horrible place where his friends, family, and colleagues question him or maybe even completely disown him. With no friends or colleagues, he looks bad and he becomes completely isolated. You have not only hurt him, but now he's vulnerable to be hurt more.

Ideally, if you are a covert manipulator, you will never reveal that you were the one who tore down his reputation. You may tear him down through rumors, or through leaking something dishonorable about his character or past. You may set him up to be wrong at a critical point so that he looks like a fool. Whatever you do, don't implicate yourself so that he knows you are responsible for what happened.

If you remain innocent in his eyes, then he may turn to you for help. He wants a friend. So you offer him a shoulder to cry on and pretend to be his friend. Now you can betray him even more. You can maneuver him to do things for you in the guise that you are trying to get him to regain his positive public image.

Make Him Question His Sanity

Messing with someone's head is something that we cover in more detail in Chapter 2. But you need to know that making someone question his own sanity will really make him vulnerable. Once he starts questioning his own mind, he won't know who to trust. He will be completely vulnerable and may turn to you for guidance about what is real. Then you have the perfect opportunity to plant ideas in his mind and mold his thinking to suit you.

Disrupt His Peace

Your subject probably really values his peace and his routine. He likes things a certain way. He relies on things being as he expects. Maybe he has a favorite coffee shop, or a quiet place where he likes to go to work or think. Maybe he needs his room totally dark and quiet in order to fall asleep. You can unsettle him and mess up his thought processes if you completely disrupt his sense of peace. You can also weaken his defenses if you disrupt his sleep or his routine.

Provoke His Anger

One final basic to manipulation is creating a situation that is unbearable to someone. You might annoy him, hurt him, embarrass him, or otherwise make him feel uncomfortable. He will do anything to get out of the situation.

You might use this to get out of a party, for instance. Pretend to be a big goofball naturally. Embarrass and annoy him until he wants to leave, just so that you can get out of the party. But pretend like you don't mean to do anything wrong, because you want to remain covert.

You can also use this tactic to make him cringe and avoid displeasing you. For instance, if he makes you mad, be sure to tell everyone about it. This makes him feel embarrassed. He will avoid making you mad in the future so that you don't make him look like a bad person.

Work very hard to find what sets him off. Everyone has a trigger for annoyance, anger, and irritation. Everyone has a limit to his or her patience. You can hit this trigger or push him to the limit, causing him to explode at you in public. Then he will seem like someone with an anger issue and other people will think badly of him. You can pretend that you are innocent and that you didn't deserve his outburst of rage.

Finally, you can use annoyance to start a fight so that you can express your own rage. You don't need to start a fight directly. Just keep annoying him until he loses his temper. This gives you a justifiable reason to get angry and tell him hurtful things. You can really destroy his ego

through a few verbal slashes.

Chapter 2: Always Get a Yes

Persuasion is one the biggest applications of manipulation. You can persuade people to do whatever you desire. Even if someone tells you no, you can turn that into a yes. You can also approach people in the correct way right off the bat, so that you never hear the word "no."

Persuasion is relatively easy. The key to persuading others is making them feel good and making them want to say yes. You basically have to inspire someone to want to do what you suggest. Sometimes, all you have to do is find a good motivating reward to get someone to do what you want. Other times, it takes a little bit more work. But it is possible to motivate people to do what you want, even they are initially unwilling.

Offer a Reward

People operate based on rewards. They often expect some sort of reward to feel motivated to do anything. To get someone to do something for you, you can offer a reward. The most common reward is monetary payment, but you might offer something else that they really want. Exchange a favor for a favor, for example.

Sometimes the only reward that people require is an emotional one. Make someone feel good. Praise is often sufficient for accomplishing this. Offer someone flattering compliments or lavish praise upon them to gain their favor and motivate them. Feeling good can motivate anyone, so use that knowledge to your advantage.

Focus on How they Benefit

When you want to persuade someone, you must sell the idea to him. The only way you can do this is if you put an emphasis on how he will benefit. He does not care so much about how you will benefit, unless he really, really loves you. Rather, he cares about himself and whether or not the effort he puts into this favor is worth the return that he will get. So try to prove to him that he will benefit greatly from doing something for you by focusing only on his benefits, not your own. Don't even bring yourself or your own needs up. Really sell the thing that you are trying to persuade him about. Glamorize it and make it seem incredibly tempting.

Foot in Door Technique

Get someone into the mode of doing things for you by asking for small, negligible favors at first. Ask for things like a buck for a soda, or help holding the door open. Once the person says yes, you put him on a track of doing things for you. He is psychologically more likely to tell you yes when you ask for a larger favor. Build up the size of favors until you get what you want.

Door in the Face Technique

This technique is a bit risky, but boisterous businessmen are often able to pull it off. You can try your luck with it. In this method, you ask someone for an outrageous favor that he is sure to say no to. Then after he says no and tries to slam the door in your face, say, "OK, you can't do that. But would you be willing to do this?" That is when you ask for your real favor. It will seem like a much smaller favor after the huge one you just requested, so he may feel relieved and think, "I can do this."

Yes Framing

You can lead someone into saying yes to you by using a method known as framing. Framing works by making someone think along certain lines. You want to frame someone to think along "yes" lines. You can do this by making someone say yes. Ask questions that are likely to get yes answers, such as, "Lovely weather today, huh?" or "Do you feel better?" Sometimes you will run into a difficult person who says no to these types of questions, so this method won't work on such people. But most people will answer yes to common questions, such as questions about the weather, so this means that people will start to think along yes lines when they answer yes more and more. Then they are more likely to say yes when you finally ask them the big question or make the request that you want.

This method can be flipped to persuade someone to say no. You want to do the reverse and ask people questions that will likely make them say no. "You don't care for this, do you?" or "Do you like being ripped off?" Ask things that most people would say no to.

Anchoring

You can convince someone that your suggestion is golden by comparing it to poorer options. People will compare options that they are presented with. If you present only bad alternative options, you can make someone feel that he must pick your option because it is the only good one.

Let's take an example. You want to make someone buy your product. So you show him other products for higher prices. Shield him from seeing the good deals out there. He will think that you offer the best price, so he agrees to buy from you and not another seller.

You can also set a really high price or make something seem like it is worth more than it is. That initial value is the anchor. When someone bargains you down, he feels that he is getting a great deal. But in reality, he is paying more than the fair price for the product or service. He doesn't know that you are the real winner here. This is a used car salesman's tactic that you can employ on your customers.

Get Someone to Make a Small Commitment

This technique works on the idea of commitment and consistency, one of the Six Principles of Influence that work for persuasion. Seldom do people vary in their behavior too drastically. Most people prefer to stick to what they know, which means that people tend to stick to behavior that they already do. This is why people will tend to follow through on commitments that they have already made instead of veering off course and making huge changes to their lives. You can use this idea to your advantage. Get someone to do something for you or to commit to something small and painless. Once they get used to the idea of doing things for you, they will probably continue to do so. This means that they will continue to serve you.

Charities often use this technique to persuade their donators to donate even more money. If someone already cares about a cause enough to donate some money every now and then, he is more likely to respond to polite letters asking for more money. He will increase his donations or make a larger donation around Christmas to the same charity. He may not do that for a different charity, however.

Use Guilt

Reciprocity is another principle of influence that you can absolutely use covertly. You want to use guilt to get people to do things for you. You can create guilt using reciprocity. Do nice things for people so that they feel as if they owe you. People like to repay favors, so they will probably want to do something for you once you do something for them. The saying "Scratch my back and I'll scratch yours" is a summary of this principle.

Panic Someone

You want to make it seem that what you are offering someone is in limited supply. Make them feel panicked that this thing that you have to sell or give will not be there forever. Show them that this thing is in high demand and therefore must be good, so they need to act fast or someone will beat them to it.

Tell people that you already have several buyers interested in the car you are selling who are willing to give you full price, for example, to make potential buyers feel pressured to buy the car before someone else does. They won't look into the Kelley Blue Book value of the car or consider its flaws because they are in a hurry to get this deal that you are offering them.

If you make someone a job offer, suggest that you have other candidates in mind as well. This way, your potential employee will feel pressured to take the job before someone else gets it. He won't take the time to evaluate the position so he might miss something bad about the job or fail to find a better opportunity.

Be an Authority

To persuade people, you have a lot more luck if you establish some sort of dominance or authority. The obvious way to do this is to be in a leadership position, or to use the endorsement of a celebrity or expert. Once you seem like an authority figure or have the backing of an authority figure, people will listen to you. This is why ads love to quote statistics or use celebrity endorsements.

But you can do this more covertly, too. You can start by often telling someone what to do. Perhaps give him advice that really works, or sell him something that works great for his needs. This establishes both authority and trust. He will rely on your opinion, services, or products again in the future. You can influence him using the authority that you have established. When you tell him to do something, he is more likely to do it.

Appearing like an authority figure, even if you are not, is also a great way to accomplish this. You can be intimidating without doing anything wrong. One of the best ways to do this is to appear taller. You can puff out your chest, correct your posture, and wear high heels or lifts in your shoes to give the illusion that you are taller. You should also speak in a deeper voice and be bossy. Fearlessly make and hold eye contact.

Be the Person People Want to Help

If you make people want to help you, then most of the work of persuasion is already completed. By appearing both likable and vulnerable, you get people to want to help. They want to be the hero. So they do what you want in the name of helping you out.

You can accomplish this by being very warm and endearing. Be the sweetest person alive. But also share a few tragic details, or open up about something personal. Offer someone a coat, warm drink, candy, or something else free to make them think that you are a warm and generous person even in your time of need. You may try using seduction tricks at this point and suggest that you might be attracted to your subject. This makes people feel that you are a victim. It also makes them think that you trust them and that you sense some sort of bond exists between you two.

Chapter 3: Using NLP and CBT to Get Your Way

To be a truly successful covert manipulator, you must be able to use some heavy duty psychological tricks on people. This way, you can influence people without being detected. Dark NLP and Dark CBT offer you a wide array of possible ways to enter someone's mind and mold someone to think the way that you want. You have limitless power over others through these psychological methods. Essentially, turning positive psychology around on people enables you to perform brainwashing in a very covert manner.

Dark Neuro-Linguistic Programming

Neuro-linguistic programming enable you to influence someone through language, body language, facial expressions, and certain subliminal techniques. Dark NLP enables you to make someone act certain ways. Your subject won't even know why he likes you so much or why he acts certain ways around you because NLP is very subliminal and obscure. Just by speaking to someone a certain way and changing a few words in your expression of a phrase can have a tremendous effect on how he responds and starts to think and act toward you.

So let's dive in now and find out how Dark NLP can really work on your subject.

Getting a Read

NLP requires for you to be observant. You want to get a good read on your subject so that you understand how to best influence him. First, observe how he speaks and notice what sensory organ he seems to use the most. This is called his sensory modal system and refers to whether he uses his visual, auditory, or tactile sense the most. Also, learn what he is passionate about and what he hates so that you know what he likes to talk about. Observe him to find out what rules he lives by and how he thinks so that you can encourage him to change these rules and live by new ones that you set. Finally, learn how he lies and how he expresses himself when he feels certain emotions. It often takes some practice and some time to get a good, clear read on someone.

Make Someone Like You

If someone likes you, he is more likely to try to please you and do what you want. Therefore, you can use NLP techniques to make someone feel attached to you. The easiest way to do this is to make someone associate you with something really pleasant that makes him happy. For instance, if he loves a certain scent, wear it or spray it in your office or home so that he associates you with that pleasant aroma. Talk about things that he loves. Praise him and tell him nice things so that you boost his ego.

You should also create a false bond by mirroring his movements and facial expressions. When you match his expressions and gestures, he will subconsciously feel that you two share a lot in common. He will trust you and like you and he won't know why.

You can also use light touch to enforce a bond. Just brushing his hand or letting your fingers linger on his when you shake hands can make him feel closer to you. People are bonded by physical touch, so this really works.

Anchors

Anchors uses the idea of conditioning. You want to anchor someone's attention on some sort of external stimulus. Then create an association with an internal feeling or thought. Later, exposing the person to the anchor will cause him to think of the thought or feeling that he has associated it with. So for example, you can touch his leg briefly when describing a sexual fantasy. Later, all you have to do is touch his leg, and he will reenter the fantasy and wonder why he is suddenly weak with desire.

Alternatively, you can make someone associate something bad with a leg touch. Then, when he is about to do something that you don't like or when he makes you angry, just touch his leg. His good mood will sour as bad thoughts flood his mind.

Sensory Modal Systems

Every person has a preferred modal system. He views the world through the lens of his preferred system. You can make a great impression on him and get him to do what you want by communicating with him using his preferred modal system.

If you want someone to go somewhere with you and he says no, describe the place to him in his modal system. For instance, if he is a more visual person, describe how nice the place looks and how much he will enjoy the views.

When selling something, you want to listen to a person's conversation to determine his or her preferred modal system. If he says "look," and "do you see what I mean" and other such visual terms, for instance, he is a more visual person. So you want to describe a product to him in visual terms to appeal to him. If he says more things like "do you hear me?" or "that sounds great!" then he is more auditory and you must appeal to him by describing how something sounds.

Speaking to someone using his preferred modal system makes communication easier, too. He will understand you more clearly if you use his preferred modal system. You can also use this tactic to deliberately create miscommunication and confusion by speaking to him in the wrong modal system.

Body Language

Your body language can really communicate a lot. When you speak to someone, you want to influence him by using certain body language. If you want to impart a more negative emotion, cross your arms, turn slightly away from him, and avoid eye contact. He will get the message and you don't have to say anything. If you want to impart a more positive message, lean into him, brush his hand or arm, put an arm around his shoulders, and make lots of eye contact while smiling warmly.

Emotional Responses

You want to invoke certain emotional responses in people to drive their behavior. Making someone feel happy can make him want to do something. You can discourage him from doing something that you don't want by invoking a negative emotion. This is why you need to find out what someone loves and hates when you are getting a read on him.

Use sensory stimulus that inspires him or makes him happy. If he is passionate about baseball, for instance, you can talk about baseball before you ask him for a favor. He will subconsciously make an association between the positive vibe he gets from the baseball conversation and the favor that you ask him. Then he will say yes.

If he is about to do something that you don't like, you can tell him, "Go for it!" Then bring up a conversation about something dreadful that will bother him. He will form an ugly association and try to avoid doing what you were just discussing.

Meta Modeling

Later on we talk about Dark CBT and how you can use it to influence people. Meta modeling is the NLP version of CBT. It encourages someone to see the error of his ways or his thinking in order to fix the problems in his life. It shows him what he is doing to create issues in his life and what he can do to change. Talk about brainwashing! You can really take advantage of meta modeling to change someone's behavior and even his personality over time.

Meta modeling suggests that people form certain rules early in life. They live by these rules, even if these rules don't serve them well and end up making their lives more messy. People cling to their rules steadfastly and faithfully. This is why most people have fairly reliable and predictable behavior. If you observe someone long enough, you will spot the rules that he lives by. He may believe that he must always be negative and hopeless, for instance, so that he is not disappointed when something doesn't work out. He may think that he must be perfect in order to please others and so he works himself too hard and criticizes himself harshly. He may also think that the world is against him, and that he is all alone.

Once you know his rules, you can exploit them. Either encourage him to keep following a certain rule if it behooves you, or encourage him to drop that rule and adopt another to live by. Scramble with his sense of order and his rules so that he tries to change his life. You can totally alter his thinking and his personality if you teach him new rules, or you can cement harmful rules that he already lives by. It really depends on what you are trying to accomplish with dark meta modeling.

Let's take this example. A guy who is a perfectionist is too hard on himself. So you can use that to your advantage and play with his rule by telling him that what he did could be better. Pretend to be pushing him to do his best, when really you're just driving him crazy by pushing him to do more and more. He will strive to please you and meet your exact standards if he lives by the belief that he must be perfect to please the people whom he loves.

Or say someone believes that he must always be alone, but you want him to depend on you. So you can show him that being alone is not healthy. Make him feel good so that he comes to love the feeling of being around someone. Challenge him to do things that he can't accomplish on his own, and jump in to give him assistance so that he learns that life is easier with your help.

When someone states a belief, he will do it in a subconscious way. He might tell you how he thinks by stating something general like, "Everyone is always the same." Challenge him when he makes a statement like this to make him reevaluate his thinking. Offer him some examples of people who are different from everyone else.

Positive Phrasing

How you phrase things is extremely important. There are often dozens, sometimes even hundreds, of ways to express the same exact message in the English language. But which way you choose to convey a certain message can really affect how the other person responds and feels.

One key part of this concept is making people respond more positively to what you say so that they do what you want. You can do this by using positive language that encourages people, rather than negative language.

A negative phrase might be, "Don't you dare cheat on me." This message is loud and clear. But guess what? It's counterproductive. That is because the human mind tends to leave off the "don't" and only pays attention to the latter part of the command. So if you say "Don't you dare cheat on me," you make the other person's subconscious mind hear and process "Cheat on me." You just influenced him to cheat on you.

So you can use this in two ways. On one hand, you can use negative phrases to make people do the opposite of what you say. For instance, if you do actually want someone to cheat on you so that you have a brilliant excuse to fight with the person or something to hold against him later on in the relationship, you might choose to tell him, "Don't cheat on me!" On the other hand, if you don't want him to cheat, use more positive language that his subconscious mind will accept. Say something like, "I know that you are a faithful and that you will stay faithful to me. I love that about you. I feel that I can trust you." See how nice that message sounds? He will appreciate the message and he will be more likely to strive to stay faithful.

You can use this same concept to influence people to adopt certain qualities in their behavior. Tell him something that you want him to do or to be. Say something like, "I know that you are a trustworthy person." This makes him think that he is trustworthy, and so he will be more honest and forthcoming with you. You encourage him to do what you want by telling him exactly what you want. Saying something like "I hope you don't lie to me" suggests that you think that he is a liar, and so he will be more inclined to lie to you.

Tell people things that you love about them. This encourages them to keep doing it to earn your praise. "I love how generous and kind you are!" is a way better message that makes someone feel good and want to keep being generous and kind. In fact, they will want to be more generous and kind, and will probably ramp up what they do for you. Telling someone, "I wish you were more generous" simply puts the person down and makes him sense that he lacks something. He will continue to disappoint you as a result.

Also, speak more in terms of gain than loss. This influences people to want to do something because they perceive some sort of reward is in store for them down the road. When you speak in terms of loss, this sounds more discouraging. Always tell people what they will gain from doing what you want, and never bring up what they must give up or stop doing.

A very common example of this is when you encourage someone to lose weight with your program. If you tell people that they will lose weight with your program, this may sound appealing, but they will probably end up quitting the program or not actually shedding any pounds because you are telling them to lose something. You are also making them think of weight loss as something restrictive that takes something from them. You instead want to tell them what they will gain with your program and what they get to do on your program. Tell them that they will gain fitness and look more beautiful if they stick with the program. Let them know that they get to do fun workouts and eat more nutritious food, rather than telling me to cut carbs and to stop being lazy.

Dark Cognitive Behavioral Therapy

Cognitive behavioral therapy is a method by which therapists or individuals can teach themselves new thought patterns and new behaviors. They identify ways that they think incorrectly, and then introduce new, more helpful ways of thinking. You can start playing therapist and teaching people to think in different ways.

Cognitive behavioral therapy addresses cognitive distortions which lie at the base of unhealthy thinking and low mood. But if you are using CBT to your own manipulative ends, you might consider encouraging cognitive distortions. You want to lead people to abandon old thinking patterns and adopt new ones. Ask people a line of questions to make them doubt the validity of their thinking and to encourage them to look at life in new ways.

First, let's talk about common cognitive distortions. Then we'll talk about how to influence thinking based on encouraging or discouraging cognitive distortions. After that, we'll cover some specific techniques for using these methods.

- **Assuming**: A person who assumes thinks that something is right without sufficient evidence. He jumps to conclusions and causes himself a lot of grief by operating on incorrect assumptions. You can suggest things to a person so that he believes them and makes an assumption based on what you say. Then he will act on that assumption and cause damage to his life or his relationships.

- **All-or-nothing thinking**: Things are either all peachy or all horrible to a person who engages in all-or-nothing thinking. This type of thinking is severely unbalanced and unrealistic. It can cause someone to set himself up for severe disappointment or to always be negative and miserable about things. You can suggest all-or-nothing types of thoughts to someone, encouraging him to develop this cognitive distortion. If he already has this cognitive distortion, encourage it further.

- **Dwelling and ruminating**: Dwelling on problems does not solve them. You can make someone avoid solving his problems by always bringing them up, keeping him from moving on or focusing on a viable solution. He stays miserable, dependent on you for help, and unable to fix his problems. His life never changes.

- **Overgeneralizing**: This is where someone thinks that everything is always the same. He puts the same labels on everyone at all times. This causes him to miss out on opportunities and make hasty judgments about people or situations that may be untrue. Telling someone that everyone hates him or that everyone is the same can teach him to start thinking this way. Expose him to overgeneralizations and eventually he will start to think this way himself.

- **Mind reading**: This cognitive distortion is where people think that they know what others are thinking. They read too much into small actions or facial expressions. They don't ask others directly what they think, but instead they assume and operate on those assumptions, even if they are wrong. Usually mind readers are not accurate. But you can make someone think that he is a mind reader by telling him that he is right when he tries to read someone's mind or by suggesting what someone might be thinking.

- **Negative self-labeling**: Negative self-labeling is the process of always blaming one's self and criticizing one's self. It leads to horrible self-esteem and also causes people to blame themselves, not you. You can cause someone to adopt this cognitive distortion by constantly criticizing him, embarrassing him, and pointing out his flaws.

- **Disqualifying the positive**: Negative nancies are people who use this cognitive distortion. A person who disqualifies the positive never sees the good in a situation and only focuses on the negative, causing depression, despair, and hopelessness. Pointing out only negative things can change someone's disposition and tear away his positivity. It can catapult him into depression and make him lose his sense of vitality and his will to do things.

- **Disqualifying the present**: A person who lives in the future or past is not able to take care of the present or feel grateful for the things that he currently has. He is haunted by a sense of discontentment, as well as impatience or regret.

- **Blaming others**: In this cognitive distortion, a person blames others for everything wrong in his life and doesn't take responsibility. You can encourage someone to think this way so that you can destroy his personal relationships and make him lash out at others.

- **"Should" thinking**: Things should have happened this way. He should have been nice to me. I should have more money. These are a few of the kinds of thoughts one might have if he buys into the cognitive distortion known as "should" thinking. Telling someone that things should be a certain way can alter his sense of happiness and disable his ability to accept life, so that he becomes discontent and frustrated. You can also damage someone's self-esteem by telling him how he *should* be.

- **Catastrophizing**: This is where a person blows things out of proportion and thinks that everything is way worse or way more dramatic than it really is. You can cause your victim to suffer lots

of anxiety and hurt if you
encourage him to freak out over
small things. You can also
permanently change his thinking
and make him develop anxiety
problems while stripping away his
sense of serenity and discernment.

- **Excessive need for approval**:
  You base your happiness on the
  approval of others and make
  decisions based on what others
  think. You strive to please,
  neglecting your own needs. A
  victim of manipulation can become
  very agreeable to your needs if you
  train him to adopt this cognitive
  distortion.

How to Use Dark CBT

The main way to use CBT is to encourage someone to keep thinking a certain way. So once you figure out what cognitive distortion someone has, you might want to encourage him to keep thinking along those lines, or you can suggest that he thinks along more helpful lines if more positive thinking will help you achieve your goal. On the other hand, if you identify a cognitive distortion that could be helpful to your ultimate goals with a subject, then you can encourage him to develop that cognitive distortion over time. Dark CBT works well and it builds up over time, teaching people to adopt certain forms of harmful thinking that disrupt their personalities and their progress in life.

When you use Dark CBT, first you want to set a clear goal. You don't want to share this goal with the subject under any circumstances. This goal is for you to know and only you to know. This is the key to being covert. To set a goal, determine just how you want to change someone's thinking. What do you want to accomplish? If you want to destroy someone's self-esteem so that he becomes dependent on you for happiness and never leaves your side, then you would want to encourage things like negative self-labeling. If you want to make someone sick with anxiety and destroy his certainty and happiness, then you might want to teach him to catastrophize.

Remember that you can also teach someone to abandon cognitive distortions and adopt more helpful thought patterns if that suits your purposes, too. If you want to motivate an employee, teach him to qualify the present and the positive so that he focuses on finding solutions and being upbeat. As a parent, you might want to teach your child to stop blaming others for his problems so that he can learn how to solve his own life issues. Read through the different cognitive distortions and determine what behooves you.

Also, read your subject. Are there any cognitive distortions that he already possesses? Almost everyone has at least one harmful thinking habit. You might want to exacerbate these distortions, or end that distortion and encourage him to think more positively. It is easier to work with what someone already has than to create entirely new types of thinking. Take advantage of harmful or good thought habits that he already possesses.

Next, you need to work toward this goal very industriously. See the list of cognitive distortions to determine different ways that you want your subject to think. Then start feeding him these thoughts or rewarding him when you notice him using a cognitive distortion. Remember that people are sensitive to the power of suggestion, so suggesting a harmful thought when he is thinking positively can really turn his thinking around. Conversely, suggesting that he thinks more positively and finds solutions to his problems can help you if you are using CBT to erase cognitive distortions in your subject.

Also use questions to make him reevaluate his thinking. Say you are trying to make someone catastrophize. He is calm about a problem at work. Start asking him, "Should you really be calm about this? I mean, you could lose your job over this. You could lose our big client. You could get a demotion or be the first victim in the layoffs. This is a big deal!" Ask him a series of questions so that he starts to think more along the lines that you desire.

You want to start the questioning by saying something like, "Do you really think that you are thinking about this in the right way?" Then suggest things by saying, "What if?"

In the case of mind reading, you don't need to use questions. Instead, suggest, "He probably thinks...." Then suggest the worst possible thing that he might be thinking. Pretend to be casual about it. If your subject gets upset, ask, "Why are you upset? I was just suggesting something that he might be thinking. You want to prepare for the worst. After all, he seemed pretty mad."

Chapter 4: Subliminal Manipulation and Conditioning

Subliminal psychology is the cornerstone of covert manipulation. This is because you are conditioning someone with images, scents, and emotional associations. He is not aware that you are conditioning him in any way. All he knows is that suddenly he feels a certain way or wants a certain thing and he does not know why.

Subliminal Mind Tricks

Subliminal Messaging

A subliminal message is something that somebody doesn't even notice. It might be a flashing image, or a brief whiff of a scent. This message infiltrates his subconscious mind, though, making him think about it.

Let's say you want to go eat at a certain restaurant. You can flash a picture of its ad on your computer screen while your subject is talking to you. Later, he will find himself craving the restaurant's food. Or you might ask him where he wants to eat, while you start walking in the direction of the restaurant in question. He will know that the restaurant is in the direction that you are heading so he will think of it.

Misdirection

You can use the classic magician's trick of misdirection to distract someone from what you are really doing. Show him something that draws his attention. Wave your hand around while you're talking, for instance, so that he pays attention to that hand and doesn't notice what the other one is doing.

Leading Questions

The way you phrase a question can lead someone to a certain answer. Frame your questions to guide someone toward a certain desired answer. Inject phrases that he is sure to agree to, or imply guilt and don't let him deny it.

For instance, you can ask someone if something is wrong, which will make him think that something must be wrong to prompt you to ask that.

Or you might ask him "What were you doing when you smashed into the other car?" which makes him tell you what he was doing because he is focused on that part of the question. Inadvertently, he forgets to deny that he smashed into the other car, so he takes on guilt.

Scotomas

Scotomas are mental blind spots where someone can't see something that is going on clearly. You can exploit these scotomas. Scotomas are often created by someone's subconscious denial of a humiliating or painful fact. You might use someone's scotoma to do things that he won't notice. You might also point out his scotomas so that he feels stupid or so that his carefully constructed world falls apart and he becomes confused and uncertain of his perception.

For instance, a guy might deny that his wife is cheating on him because it humiliates him deeply, so you can use that denial to your advantage to get away with an affair with his wife. He will never guess because he is choosing to be blind to her infidelity.

He might also fail to realize that the office avoids him because he talks too much. When you point this out, he will start to notice it. Then his self-esteem will take a huge plummet.

Reverse Psychology

Tell someone that he can't do something, and he will do it. He won't even guess that you are goading him to do what you really want because you told him that you don't want him to do that. Parents use this a lot with their kids. A parent might tell his kid, "You can't have any spinach," as everyone eats it in front of him. His kid will decide that he wants spinach just because he's been told that he can't have it.

You can use this on someone by telling him that you don't really need his help so that he jumps in and helps in order to feel needed, or you might tell him that he can't get a certain girl so he goes after her just to prove you wrong.

Priming

Make someone fall into a good mood or a bad mood to influence the decision that he makes. For instance, if he is about to make a big purchase, you can bring up a decision or topic that fills him with doubt or joke about that time he made a terrible decision. This doubtful mood will leak into his purchase decision, making him indecisive. Or you can put him in a bad mood by bringing up something dark from the past, talking about a depressing news story, or flashing a negative and disturbing image in front of his eyes briefly. He won't be so elated about the purchase and he might not make it because he has now associated the product with feeling bad. If you want him to buy something for you, you can put him in a great mood and then ask him to make the purchase.

Conditioning

Conditioning works by training someone to react to a certain trigger. You expose someone to a trigger whenever he does something. Then later, whenever he is exposed to that trigger, he will perform the associated action. Conditioning can take a while to take hold, but it is a very deep and undetectable means of getting someone to comply with your wishes.

One way to condition someone is to always reward him for doing something with a pleasurable action, praise, or a reward. Soon, the minute you tell him something sweet or give him a gift, he automatically does whatever it is that you are conditioning him to do.

You might play a certain song someone likes when he cleans the house. From then on, whenever you play that song, he will want to clean. He's made an association between the song he likes and cleaning. Cleaning is suddenly more pleasurable to him and he will be more willing to do it.

You may also use something such as a sound, scent, or image to condition someone over time. Soon he will do what you want the minute he sees the stimulus that you have conditioned him with. It's as simple of showing him the color yellow to get him to go work out, for instance.

Chapter 5: Being Covert and Stealthy

As the titles of this book indicates, being discreet about your manipulation is key to its success. You are learning how to become a covert manipulator, which means that you should never get caught. The methods contained in this book are all pretty stealthy. There are some manipulation methods that have been omitted simply because they are so obvious. You might run across some of these methods in other books or online. You want to avoid using these methods. Covert manipulation is a thousand times more successful than obvious manipulation. If you are never caught, then no one will ever be able to accuse you of manipulation and your reputation will remain impeccable.

The most covert method covered in this book are the subliminal methods. These methods are very clandestine. No one will be able to detect them. To be a true covert manipulator, you want to work in this underhanded way.

But subliminal methods don't always work in every situation.

Wear a Mask

You want to create a mask that everyone will see. Your true intentions will never show through this mask. What you create for others to see is really up to you. Some people like to create a victim mask, where they act as if they are the ones being hurt. Others like to create a charming façade that is infectious and irresistible. Yet others like to put on a blither and innocent façade, and act as if they are completely clueless about how harmful they are to others.

Find the façade that works best for you. It should be the way that you find easiest to act. It may even incorporate parts of yourself that you like, or elements that you wish you possessed in your true personality. Create a façade that you love. This is your way of recreating yourself.

Be Very Charming

Charm is the key to getting people to like you and to open up to you. Charm is a natural part of one's personality, but you can turn up the charm with a few techniques. The first is that you want to be gracious and to remember things about people. Offer a big smile and lots of compliments. Touch people lightly to encourage a bond to form. Tell a good, clean joke. Offer to take someone's coat or hat, or to walk the person to his or her car. Having manners and being chivalrous is both rare and incredibly charming, so it will work for you well. You should also have a slightly removed air, as if you are a bit distant or off in your own world. This makes you mysterious without being rude. People will wonder what you are thinking about and they will try to get closer to you. Finally, keep up your appearance to add to your charm and try your best to always look good. People are best attracted to those who make an effort and have confidence in their outward appearances.

Act Innocent

You don't want to be overly sneaky when you are being covert, or you give away your position. You instead want to act like you are doing nothing wrong and you have full confidence in the innocence of your actions. If you act like you are doing nothing wrong, people will assume that you are in the right. Only when you act guilty or sneaky do people start to get suspicious.

Keep a Good Reputation

Appear like a great person. That way, others can't get away with accusing you of wrongdoing. If you have a clean and impeccable reputation and don't get caught manipulating people, then you are more likely to get away with manipulation in the future. You want to make people think that you are harmless and even a good person. You also want them to think that you couldn't possibly mean them any harm.

It is also best to get lots of people to like you. The more well-liked that you are, the more likely people will want to spend time with you. They will be less likely to reject you or avoid you. And you will be able to get them to do what you want because they will want to befriend you and please you.

Compliment More than You Hurt

We covered how to build people up and then tear them down as part of manipulation and emotional abuse. But if you want to be covert, you want to seem like a better person than you really may be. Therefore, you want to offer more positive encouragement and love than discouragement. You want to compliment people more than you hurt them.

Basically, you want to make people like you and feel good around you. Then you make them dependent on you. They won't know why they like you so much. But they will rely on you for ego bolstering, which is why they can't get enough of you. You can gain control in this way and appear perfectly innocent and even nice.

Disguise Your Insults

Pretend to only hurt someone because you care about them. This is the classic mother trick. You might tell someone that he can't succeed at something, but this is only because you don't want to see him fail. You might tell someone that he has a flaw, but it's only to prevent him from making a fool of himself. Disguising your abuse as kindness is a great way to be covert.

You can always pretend to always mean well. If your intentions seem pure, your actions are more excusable. You can get away with more.

Blame it on Someone Else

The best way to do this is to pin the blame on the victim of your manipulation. You can make someone feel bad about the bad things that you do to him! This clever twist-around enables you to beat your victim down more while maintaining your innocence. Tell him that he deserved what happened to him or that he makes you act in certain ways. Make him feel as if his personality and his actions are the root cause of what you do to him. Don't ever say sorry or make him feel that you are the one to blame. He needs to blame himself at all times.

You can also blame others. Say your partner is mad because he thinks that you lied to him. You can tell him that he is just paranoid because his ex lied to him a lot so now he has trust issues.

Or you can make it seem like someone else is responsible for what you did. Frame another person for your actions. This beautifully disguises your guilt while pitting two people against each other.

Chapter 6: Guard Yourself against Manipulation and Emotional Abuse

No one likes being manipulated. When manipulation occurs, you lose your power and your will. You must do what the other person wants. You often have no idea what the other person is really planning and you have no say in the situation. This makes life very difficult and it can cause you to do things that you don't want to do.

Now that you know the secrets to covert manipulation, you also know what to watch out for. You can reverse the techniques in this book to see when others are manipulating you. You can also flip these tactics on people and give them the manipulation that they are trying to run on you. There are various ways that you can protect yourself against manipulators.

Identify when You are a Victim

Everyone has a gut instinct that rears up when they are being used or misguided. Your gut instinct is very sound. You will know when you are a victim. The problem is, a lot of people ignore their instincts. You might ignore yours. You might think something like, "I'm just being paranoid" or "What could possibly go wrong if I hang out with this person?" You might think that the harm will be worth the benefits that you could get from knowing this person who gives you bad vibes. Maybe everyone else likes this guy, so you think that you are just being weird and you should like him too. Or maybe he is able to charm you and convince you that he is not so bad and over time you start to get over your

initial bad vibes.

But vibes are not something that you
should ever ignore. The minute your gut warns
you about someone, listen. Your first impression
of someone is never wrong. If you get a bad first
impression, don't give the person a second
chance. You know more about someone by just
glancing at them than you would think. The
human brain is amazingly powerful; you only are
conscious of roughly ten percent of your brain,
so there is a lot going on under the surface that
you are not consciously aware of. Your brain is
capable of reading people and determining the
future far more than you realize.

So when you get that gut feeling,
understand that your brain is working very hard

and noticing things that you are not consciously aware of. The person that you get bad vibes may not be matching his body language to his words, or he may be acting oddly in ways that you can't detect easily. Listen to your gut!

If you are just not in touch with your gut at all, or if you have doubts about someone, you might want to consider looking at some other signs. You can identify a manipulator based on his actions and language choices. You can also tell by how you feel around this person. There are various clues that point out who someone really is and what his intentions are.

What Makes You Vulnerable

You may wonder why manipulators are attracted to you, especially if you have had

multiple encounters with manipulative types.
You may also wonder what you should change
about yourself to avoid running into a
manipulator in the future.

One thing that makes you vulnerable is
being accepting of manipulative treatment and
emotional abuse. If you were emotionally abused
or repressed as a child, this type of treatment
may seem normal to you. You don't know
anything else. You don't how a healthy
relationship is supposed to feel. So you accept
the terrible treatment that others would not
think of accepting. As a result, you are projecting
a sense of vulnerability that draws manipulators
from far away. The minute you begin to tolerate
their treatment and keep them in your life, they
gain power over you and choose to keep using

you until they get what they want. Work on increasing your self-esteem and avoiding familiar patterns. If you get that eerie sense of déjà vu when you meet someone, you might want to avoid that person because he is probably reminding you of previous abusive patterns that you have been in.

Another thing that may make you vulnerable is neediness or weakness. If you are in a vulnerable time in life, you might be more open to manipulators. Manipulators can see that you are in need and they see it as an opportunity to offer you what you need in exchange of what they really want. They will use any opportunity to gain control over you, and when you are in a bad period of life, you basically hand them opportunities. You need to guard your heart and mind especially well when you are at a disadvantage. Be wary of extremely kind strangers or life savers. Not all heroes are good guys. Your heroes may help you, but they may have hidden intentions. Most people won't do something for free so watch out.

You may also be a target for manipulation if you have low self-esteem. Events in your life or your childhood may have stripped away your self-esteem and confidence. You may be emotionally vulnerable. So you want people who build up your ego. Manipulators can spot this and they will move in on you, working hard to please you and make you smile. They see a way into your mind through your bruised ego. Try to build your self-esteem by yourself and work on loving yourself.

But the unfortunate truth is, everyone is a potential victim. A manipulator will see the slightest opening in your psyche and move right in. Manipulators are skilled opportunists who shamelessly go after anyone that they can. If you fall prey to a manipulator, don't feel bad and don't blame yourself. It could happen to anyone. It is not your fault. The fact that you may become a victim is why you need to read this chapter and learn how to protect yourself.

Signs of a Manipulator

A manipulator is often incredibly superficial. This means that he looks good on the outside, but there is nothing to follow it up on the inside. He is shallow and lacks depth. Everything he does and says is fake, part of a façade that he erects to fool you. So beware of people who are incredibly charming and attractive when you first meet them. Get to know them before you start confiding in them or trusting them. Don't make a commitment or business deal until you are absolutely sure of yourself.

Another sign of a manipulator is that you feel compelled to confide in him or to do what he wants. You constantly find yourself saying yes when you want to say no. It's impossible to be yourself and to stand up for yourself. He has some sort of power over you that you can't resist. Unfortunately, this power is just a carefully woven web of manipulation, deception, and emotional harm. He will dump you the minute he gets all that he can from you, so don't stick around or make the mistake of thinking that this relationship will last. He does not care, no matter how well he pretends to. Get away from him before the relationship gets too harmful and he ruins your life.

You may also find yourself saying sorry all of the time. Your guilt eats you up. Every situation with this person seems like your fault. Even if he is at fault, he manages to twist things around so that you feel guilty. He will never take responsibility for anything that he does and he will always put everything on you. He can do what he wants, but he holds you to exacting standards and punishes you when you don't follow suit. He basically kills your self-esteem and causes you to hate yourself.

Finally, a manipulator is great at changing your mind. You might feel one way, but after talking with him, you feel a completely different way. He is able to change your mind and your way of thinking. Sometimes this may even be a good thing, as he makes you think more constructively or positively. But be wary of someone who has so much power over your moods and your thoughts.

What Manipulation Feels Like

Often, in the early stages of a manipulative or emotionally abusive relationship, you will feel amazing. Your manipulator will be an expert at making you feel good about yourself. He will flatter you and fuel your ego.

Some people out there will make you feel good because they genuinely love you. But it often takes times for such a relationship to build. If someone whom you barely know is suddenly super into you and trying to rush a relationship, become very wary. Don't let things move too quickly. Get to know the person first. Someone who wants you so badly right off of the bat is usually superficial and just trying to prime you into a victim. Don't fall for it. Normal people don't just jump into relationships or try to rush things. Normal people also don't start acting crazy about you in an unusually short period of time.

A manipulator will make you feel like there are butterflies in your stomach. You will strive to please him. Your biggest desire will be to make him smile. This is because he is already making you feel as if you owe him or as if you like him so much that you will work to please him. Beware of people who make you feel like a puppet. You should never want to bend over backwards for someone so urgently. You need to have a sense of dignity and personal space and value in every relationship. If you don't, something is off.

You will also feel guilty about the smallest things. You may feel inadequate or guilty for not always pleasing this person every day. A sense of guilt about living or being you may haunt you. You may feel ashamed of who you are. These feelings may seem to come out of the blue, but this is just because you are with a super covert manipulator. Trust me, he is playing some serious games with your heart to inspire your guilt. These feelings are not random or spontaneous, but rather part of your manipulator's carefully crafted plan to hurt you. So you should become suspicious and understand that these feelings are not a normal element of a healthy relationship.

Your self-esteem will certainly dive when you spend time around a manipulator. Soon, your confidence will become riddled with holes. You will be poisoned with self-doubt and angst. This is not a good thing and you should not stay around someone who does this to you.

You also will probably start to feel crazy. You will wonder if you have an undiagnosed disorder or if you are falling apart at the seams. When you argue with this person, he will deny everything that he just said. He will call you nuts for arguing with him or claim that you are just making things up. In addition, he will invent elaborate stories and blame you for things that you never did, often so convincingly that you start to believe that you did what he claims. He will also challenge your perception of reality, lie through his teeth, and make you question yourself constantly. All of these things combined will tear at your self-esteem and consciousness, making you question your sanity. Manipulators can actually rewire the neurons of your brain and do permanent damage to your mental health and personality, so you should not stick around.

One great piece of advice is that if you feel the need to record someone during arguments because he denies what he says later and makes you feel crazy, then you are in an emotionally abusive relationship and you should leave now.

You are not crazy. This person is just gaslighting you.

What to Do when Someone is Manipulating You

The simplest piece of advice on how to deal with a manipulator is to just up and leave. If you can do this, great. You should immediately. There will be no good to come from this relationship, so why stay around and get hurt?

But this advice is often easier said than done. There are some situations where you cannot escape a manipulator and his traps. For instance, you might have to work with a manipulator and you can't just quit your job, or you don't want to. Or you might have a manipulative family member and you can't cut him off or you will lose all of your family. You may feel trapped and unable to leave for various reasons, such as financial reasons. Maybe you have kids with the manipulator and must speak to him or her for the rest of your life regarding the children. Co-parenting doesn't automatically end when your children turn eighteen; sometimes, you have to continue a relationship with the father or mother well into your children's' adult lives, and you must be around each other for your children's weddings, graduations, grandchildren, etc. Or maybe there is a manipulative friend in your group whom everyone else likes. There are countless reasons why you may be stuck with a manipulator in your life. Leaving is not always a viable option.

That is OK. Because you can easily handle manipulators.

The first step is to limit contact with the person. Avoid him as much as you reasonably can. Limiting contact allows him less time to toy with your mind. Try to add sources of joy to your life so that you can escape his negativity and start to feed your soul. Take some time to yourself so that you can recover from the harm that comes with interactions with this monster.

The second step is to plan your escape. Maybe you can't escape now. But if you develop a plan and watch out for opportunities to escape this person, you can start to prepare yourself for freedom. An end may be in sight. Make it a goal to leave this person behind in life as soon as possible. Take steps toward your goal each day.

Only in a few cases can you never, ever escape a manipulator, so if you stick to your plan to get away, you will eventually. Life changes and people move on. You won't be trapped in this situation forever. Keep your chin up and keep your eyes on the end goal.

The third step is to avoid buying into his games. Say he tries to gaslight you. Don't start arguing with him, crying, acting out in anger, or recording him to prove that you are right. Just shrug and say, "OK." He won't like how easily he won the game because he likes the fight and he likes upsetting you. Don't ever show him that he upset you, because that is how he truly wins. Instead, swallow your pride and tell him that he is right. He will soon get bored and move on to his next victim. Then you won't have to deal with him anymore.

The fourth step is to avoid doing what he really wants. You might let him win arguments, but you don't have to do what he tells you. Say he tries getting you to break up with someone. You can tell him that he's right and you will break up with this person – but then never do. It will drive him crazy that he doesn't have control over you. He will hate that you do whatever you want. Or let's use another example: he decides to pout and embarrass you at a party so that you'll leave early and do what he wants. Just ignore him with a smile on your face. Don't leave the party until you are good and ready. You can even keep telling him, "Yes, we'll leave!" but then don't. Being nice rather than combative will disarm him and keep him from fighting you, while you continue to do what you want and not what he wants.

He might try to hurt you to punish you for not doing what he wants. He might discredit you, or tell you things that deeply wound you. Don't let him get to you. Determine to move on and repair the damage. Start working on recovery right away. Being resilient like this will repel him. He will see that you are not an easy victim and he will move on to someone who is. When he starts picking at you, trying to trigger your anger or sadness, just ignore it or respond to him nicely and don't fall for the trap. Try to prove to others that you didn't do what he claims as well.

Another tactic he will use is making you seem crazy to others. If you keep a cool head and don't follow his games or his sick reasoning, you will avoid appearing crazy to others. Be as innocent as you can be. Keep an impeccable reputation and be nice to others. Eventually, people will see the truth. Even if your reputation is already damaged, you can still mitigate the damage by being the best version of yourself possible. You will win over some people at least, and kill his goal of making you look terrible.

Block Someone's Access to Your Mind

Your mind is more vulnerable than you think. Everyone is sensitive to suggestion, so you can easily fall prey to manipulators without meaning to. But you also have more power over your own mind than you think. You can guard your mind and block the attempts of manipulators.

The best way to block your mind is to gain a healthy sense of self-love and self-confidence. If you believe in yourself, you won't let others mess with your sense of self-worth and happiness. You won't fall for the tricks and self-esteem games of manipulators. Talk to yourself nicely, as if you are your own best friend. Treat yourself to nice things or spa trips or other experiences. Tend to your needs as a priority and don't feel bad about being selfish sometimes. You should come first. Your needs matter and you matter. Remember this always. A lot of people have low self-esteem and feel bad about taking care of themselves, which makes them vulnerable to cutthroat manipulators and con artists.

Another way is to whip out a recording device or start writing down what someone says to you. You should use this tactic with people who often try to gaslight you. Do it with a smile on your face. Say, "We have often had miscommunication in the past, so I want to make sure that I catch exactly what you say for later." This will make a manipulator incredibly nervous. But if you're nice about it, you can avoid a fight and disarm him.

Having witnesses around is also a good idea. He will be less likely to attack your mind with other people around. Always keep yourself armed with friends. Don't go anywhere alone with him. If you find yourself alone with him, be sure to leave at the first opportunity.

You should carefully and closely guard your personal business. Don't reveal too much to many people. Get to know someone really well and measure his sincerity over time based on how he treats others before you start to reveal things like what you love, what you hate, or what you are guilty about. Trust is precious and you shouldn't trust many people, especially those who seem very trustworthy when you first meet them. Manipulators can fool you so don't make hasty judgments about someone's good character.

When someone tries to mess with your mind, just tell them with a smile, "Don't do that." He will try to deny doing anything wrong and may even call you crazy. Just don't respond to those antagonistic efforts. You called him out, he knows that what he was doing was wrong, and now you can move on with your day. Soon he will realize that he can't get to you or make you doubt yourself.

You can also turn the tables on someone by doing the opposite of what he wants. For instance, if he tries to bring you down, just tell him that you prefer to stay positive and try to inspire him to stay positive too. If he tries to make you doubt yourself, tell him that you are comfortable with who you are. If he wants to complain and ruin something, just tell him that you are actually having a nice time and he should try to enjoy himself too. Don't fight him, but don't do what he wants either. This will drive him crazy and eventually make him back down. You may even make a positive difference in his attitude. Not all manipulators mean to be terrible people; many of them simply don't know how to get what they want in healthy ways.

When someone tries to tear you down by being insulting, you can smile and say, "Wow, I never thought about myself like that. But we all have flaws. I can definitely understand things from your perspective, too." He will be shocked and disarmed that he can't get to you. Your willingness to blithely accept what he says without getting combative will throw him off.

Set an example by being a good person to yourself and to others. This will enable you to block a lot of manipulation attempts. Manipulators simply won't be able to tarnish your reputation or bring you down. They won't be able to get a rise out of you or make you appear crazy when they goad you to desperate acts of anger.

Use Manipulation Back on Someone

One great trick is to use manipulation on someone who is manipulating you. Turn the tables on them. Make their plans fail as you covertly work to undermine their goals in manipulating you. Pretend to do what they want, and secretly mess up the whole plan. Or use their manipulation as means to get what you really want. You may or may not choose to be covert about the whole thing. It depends on how much you want to annoy or punish the person.

There are countless ways to do this. You need to observe the situation and plan accordingly. Use the tactics you learned throughout the previous chapters to find a way to covertly manipulate this person into doing what you want, while letting him think that he is getting his way with you.

Here are a few examples of things that you can do:

Someone immature in your office is spreading rumors about you. When you hear these rumors about yourself, laugh and say, "That's funny, coming from him." When the other person asks why you say that, start a rumor of your own. Tell people how they can't believe anything he says because of something ugly from his own past. Dig up some dirt on him and expose him for who he really is, or make up something that everyone will believe.

Your mother-in-law likes to make you feel guilty so that you bring the grandkids over more often. She uses various tactics to make you feel like dirt and is over-involved in your relationship with her child. Confronting her is not an option because she will blow up at you and cause problems in your marriage. So you can bring the kids over, but you make the visit as unbearable as possible. Don't discipline the children and let them wreak havoc in her house. Feed them tons of sugar before the visit so that they are extremely naughty and hyper. Maybe bring them as late as possible, when she is too tired to be patient and they are tired too so they whine and throw tantrums. If you go out to eat, take them somewhere that they hate so that they complain, cry, and refuse to eat. She won't want them to come over as much. She may also eventually lose her temper and discipline them harshly, which you can use as an excuse to make your spouse mad at her and cause a rift in the relationship so that you don't have to tolerate her demands anymore.

A manipulative friend likes to hurt you with little digs. "You have such pretty hair today for once!" is an example of the barbed insults that she will throw at you to hurt you. Instead of confronting her directly, you can pull the same trick. Smile at her and say things like, "Thanks! Your hair could use work, though. You should try my stylist." Hurt her right back but don't do it obviously.

Someone wants to ruin a party so that everyone will pay attention to her and do what she wants. So you let her ruin the party. Pay attention to her. But turn it into negative attention. Make everyone start to criticize her. Embarrass her with hurtful jokes about herself. She will think that you are giving her what she wants – until you're not. She will quickly learn not to mess with you because you have even better ammo.

You notice that a businessman is trying to "yes frame" you by asking you questions with yes answers. So turn it around by only saying no. Or start asking him your own line of questions to throw him off. It will kill the sale and help you avoid a regrettable purchase.

These are just some of many examples of how you can turn manipulation around on someone. You need to analyze the situation and find out how you can play games right back.

Conclusion

So now you're a covert manipulator. You have all of the tools necessary to begin manipulating others and getting your way. But you also have the tools to avoid being manipulated and to protect yourself from other covert manipulators. Being able to manipulate people gives you the added advantage that you can spot and deflect manipulators.

Not everyone is perfect. Most people use manipulation. It is a very efficient and useful tool to get what you want. How much and why you use manipulation is ultimately up to you. You can use it for good or for evil.

Be careful to not wear out your welcome. A little bit of manipulation goes a long way. It is best to reserve manipulation for when it is harmless, or when it will get you something that you can't get through directness. Save it for those times when you don't have any better options. You don't want to overuse it, or it will lose its power.

Nevertheless, you know have the key to unlimited power. You can enter someone's mind and bend their will to suit your purposes. You can transform a no into a yes, or vice versa. You can accomplish anything that you want. The implications of this power are huge. Think about how much easier life will be, now that you know how to get what you want.

Life is never easy. Usually, it's other people who create the most hurdles and problems for you. Conflicts of interest and personality clashes can make life far more difficult than it needs to be. A weak person will give up, but a strong and powerful person will persevere in any way possible. Covert manipulation is a great way to undermine the power of others and take power for yourself. You will emerge the victor if you use these stealthy tactics to manipulate others to do what you want.

So what are you waiting for? Start being a covert manipulator today. You will be amazed at how drastically your life will change when you start to use the techniques that you have just learned. You are on the road to a new form of life that will be much easier.